Femme Fierce

Flashes of Courage

Femme Fierce: Flashes of Courage

This publication is designed to provide information in regard to the subject matter covered. In so doing, neither the publisher nor the author is engaged in rendering legal, accounting, or other professional services. If you require legal advice or other expert assistance, you should seek the services of a professional specializing in the particular discipline required.

While the author has made every effort to provide accurate information at the time of publication, neither the publisher nor the author assumes any responsibility for errors, or for changes that occur after publication.

FIRST EDITION
Photography and Cover Design by Heidi M. Gress

A Note from Mary

Thank you for sharing your time with me.
Thank you for reading poetry.
I hope that it inspires you
to be courageous
and fierce.

Know that you are Love.

It would be wonderful to continue our conversation!

For deeper insight into each poem or if you would like to read the companion guide to many of these selections, please go to my blog on my website. I have posted personal anecdotes, explanations and prose renditions of many of these poems, including the time and setting that inspired each one to come to life.

If you would like to receive beautiful photos with extracts from these poems, please follow me on Instagram and Pinterest.

For daily inspiring and empowering messages follow me on Twitter or Facebook.

If you would like to receive special promotions, invitations to personal appearances and special events please join the mailing list on my website.

Website: MaryGiuseffi.com

Instagram: Straight Up With a Twist 2014

Facebook, Twitter, Pinterest: Mary Giuseffi

Please go to Amazon.com for a copy of my #1 Best Seller *Straight Up With a Twist*.

Let's stay in touch!!!

Sending you Love and Light,
Mary

Foreward

It came to me the other day when I was thinking about courage. I realized that for most of us, courageous acts occur in flashes. Most heroic decisions are instantaneous. The stamina and perseverance to follow through on each of our transformational epiphanies is the glue that keeps our moment of bravery intact.

There are many types of courage. Most involve risk...physical, emotional, intellectual, spiritual and psychic. Tender or tragic, flashes of courage involve matters of love and relationship. Most acts of courage are born out of passion and often times are catalyzed by a singular event which is prefaced with long periods of personal trauma or sudden acts of danger to ourselves or someone or something we care for deeply. It is in a split second, almost an out of body experience, we witness ourselves lunge forward, harnessing the extraordinary spirit, power and will to act daringly, to engage fiercely, and to call up the legacy of our collective authentic feminine. It only takes one brave moment, for an entire destiny to be forever changed. We have had enough. There is no one to save this soul but me. Courage requires faith and fierceness. Sometimes courage takes the form of play. To act like a child is to cast off the vestitures of adulthood and risk pure joy. To be courageous is to be vulnerable.

Earlier this year, I was invited to perform at an event, showcasing my poetry publically for the first time in 35 years. I had prepared a beautiful poem included in this collection. After arriving, my spirit kept gnawing at me... whispering into my soul "finish the piece you started...it is time. Write it down." And so I did, performing "Femme Fierce" unrehearsed and raw to packed auditorium. It was a flash of courage that changed the course of the entire evening. This collection was born that evening and so was my title, reclaimed to myself, poet and muse.

Femme Fierce is a collection of poetry describing flashes of courage over centuries, lifetimes, moments and legacies. As women, we can all think back to moments when we witnessed acts of great courage by our grandmothers, mothers, lovers, sisters, friends and children. We hear the stories passed down. We reflect upon our own flashes of courage. These choices redefine our lives and create the legacies we live and leave to future generations. Legacy is born from acts of courage in all matters of the heart. Courage revolts against fear. Courage is Love in action.

Mary Giuseffi
Marina Del Rey
September 2015

Femme Fierce: Flashes of Courage

Femme Fierce

I am fierce
she laughed
pen in hand

I am femme
she laughed
toast in hand

I am fierce, our grandmother's whispered,
as they knitted their socks and bobbed their hair,
and showed their gartered legs escaping to a secret life
where they dreamed of chasing a fire in their bellies
that could not be extinguished
by
famine or plague
or the plain fact,
that their vote did not count

I am fierce,
my father's mother shook her daughter
as she boarded the boat
to leave her lesser circumstances
with money still pinned in her hem from years of sewing,
by meager light in a factory with dirty air
so that her daughter might someday learn to read in
English
and breath the satisfied sigh of being seen and heard

I am femme
said my mother
who drank her disappointments in a flute
As I curtsied and poured tea in my pristine pleated blouse
she prayed and lit candles
Please, let my daughter walk through the door of
opportunity and finally take the jug from my hand

Untie my daughter from my swaddled hip
unravel the feet for centuries bound and crippled
by slavery and seduction
We know better
In the name of fashion and style
we have been reminded of our worth less ness

From the fields of bartering her good name to feed her
family
as she shies from the hand of her handlers,
She walks back to the village
never taking her eye from the horizon

I am fierce I will travel I will run, I will walk
As long as it takes
To get where I am going

Seen and Heard

We have been carved
in the wombs of the ancients
carrying water
on their head
toward the flood.
For
Womankind
over coals
barefoot,
they carry their destiny upon their heads.
Balanced so regally
Is the crown of her entrapment
With grace in her soul
over icy hot
torment
I am fierce, she chanted in time
I am femme, she cried to the Divine

I will travel I will run I will walk
As long as it takes
To get where I am going

Seen and Heard

I am fierce,
She lay lifeless and scattered
in backrooms
where hangers had more uses than we shutter
to think.
Not able to bear the wait of one more mouth to feed
She lay dying
so that we
may be

Seen and Heard

Fierce
in the face
of centuries
Ravages of war
The body politic claimed
Its heroines

It is time my daughters,
Rise up
dance the Divine
design the robes of your destiny
In golden threads and laces
gilted but not guilty

Daughters, say,
I am fierce
The ancients are with me
The mantle has been passed down
I am femme.

I am finally free to proceed beyond the boundaries of
mortality

I will travel I will run I will walk
As long as it takes
To get where I am going

Seen and Heard

The elder's work is done.
And yours, my daughters,
femme fierce
your work
has just begun

Burning Man

Dust
to
dust
Space
to
space
Breathe
to
breath
less
Heart
to
heart
less
Love
to
love
less

You

Skin
to
skin
Rapture
to
enraptured
Undone
to
done in
robes of cotton
thread
to
thread
bare

Bind me as you have done so many times
This time to your soul
You have
my string
tethered to your restless self

Sweat
to
sweat
less
Limb
to
limb
less
Embrace
to
un
embraceable

Lights on
Lights off

I have loved you
with an everlasting
love
On the playa

Where
we
all
wade
in
Simply
Dust to dust...

Shall we dance to our wakeful dreaming
or march to our matrix mind?
Frolic in loves fragile favor

or
let fortune fade to day?
Where we are rendered simply
Dust to dust

Love in Action

If I risk
Love
I awaken
the notion
that we
are
worthy
of a destiny
of joy
and
desire,
and accept
that your heart
has already broken open
for my sorrows.

Salty saintly
sisters and brothers
let the olive branches caress not strike you
Love
is the being that
emerges.

It is the timid shy light
of humanness in the face of
God.
A holygram,
this metaphor
for metamorphosis
transcendence and transformation
for even the most wretched banal beautiful being
is full of Grace.

When love speaks
listen
with the magnitude of your tremor and tears.

Finger paint
with the dew of your Soul Celebration
on a sky that is no stranger to your longing.

This aria of angelic harmony has rocked you to sleep
throughout the
eons of your lifetimes.

Paint it on your heart
with the sacred blood of the saints' whispers
who lead on you the endless journey
of falling in love with yourself.

At the first breadth
and
the last sigh
of each sun cycle
I pray to you Divine, Holy One
for the enlightened pathway
my soul's journey in this strange paradise
Love In Action.

I am in love with you
Not because I am capable
of understanding the mystery that launches ships and
topples lesser
intellects.
I am in Love with you
because my love is more perfect than what I say,
more durable than I do,
more authentic, passionate and brave than my fleeting
and paralyzing
fear.

My tears are born from wakefulness
streams of hope ful ness
will not cease.
And in a singular flash of courage

the entire world gathers as one.
I am aligned with my God in your arms
and truly know that I am love
in the fullness of all time, instantly and eternally.

You see,
to be in love
in the plainness
of ordinary days,
is to be in love
with the Infinite.

The Lost Woman

Slips
through the
wisdom well.
Fell from the crease
into
the
crevices
of
soul
less
ness.
Blue eyes turn cloudy.
Faded freak once fancying,
confused
getting fine
with
being fine.
Now she's got neither.

Slips
through
the side walk
cracks
into
the bastion of brutal.
Should I give her chalk
to create her outline?
She could lay in it like
it
was
her
home
less
ness.

There

the shadow of the young souls
and well wisher fishermen
who harvested her beauty
sucked dry like an oyster
chocked on the pearls
imparted the mystic's tea
vanished into the nameless streets.
No more to offer them.
She was trampled
into
the
Strand.

Slippery sad eyed hollow
ranting sidewalk sister
dweller of the home less kingdom
of the former beautiful.
Slipped through
stole from,
saturated by the sun
and
star shine
till her dreams turned to dust
and
her eyes were burnt out into hollow chambers of the rant.

Mice scramble where her mind danced.
All her friends are the ones she met today.
Bare backed and bruised
choosing a protector
that could not protect her
from himself.
Shares the dream pipe.

One day
she will slip
through the knot
of herself

and
hang
out to dry.

No one will miss her.

Reborn

Being a warrior
is
less
about
carrying a weapon
and
more
about
becoming a weapon

Betty Grable's Lament

I wonder if the pin up girl
feels the tacks going in,
or is she still numb
from the blur
of all those right hands
saluting her.

See,
it's my soul
you need to squeeze.
Leave my breasts for other imaginings.
And for the fitters
whose job it is to
mercilessly manipulate
my entire destiny
into this beaded jail house frock.

No Pinterest

Wasn't no Pinterest to pin our memories on
Just pricked our fingers
fell delirious
Awaited our prince
in steel and leather corsets
Left to rest upon thorns we could not feel
Grace to the wine and roses
Our current addiction to the beautiful

Pierced each other with match lit needles of our
obsessions
Seared our lust for life
as tattoos in circular mind files
Licked the dark horses at midnight
Awoke in white frocks of the dawn
Maypole dancing in steamy July

Making a living in the Madison Avenue slave trade
5'8" and a bit curvier than I should be
Mining for diamonds with the children of a lesser god
She told me to take off my cross
I told her to take my name off her list

Slept under my piano
Safe from the white noise and carbon
Played for days without pause
Practiced scales and arpeggios
Offered apologies and applause
Palmists and soothsayers looking through my peephole
None wiser for my admissions

Harm no one
Claim nothing as your own
Save the tears of my soul
I finger painted upon the hairless chests
Of the pretty boys all in a row

Virginia Doesn't Live Here Anymore

Virginia doesn't live here any more
Told her to take her fishnets and wide eyes somewhere
else
Don't need to strip tease to taste the hi life
Just need enough guts to put the glass down
Looking glasses can be tricky
Don't get that narcissus
Virginia doesn't live here any more
Told her to take a walk on somebody else's wild side
My sneakers need retreading and my stilettos let me
touch the sky

So
Why would I need to
fall in love for fifteen minutes
Already been famous in someone's eyes
She ain't no fool accept when she wants to be
and she loves the game when the stakes are high enough
But free falling isn't all its cracked up to be
Can't let that red lipstick define my lines anymore

Don't remember all the story
Praying to a higher God is this fallen angel
And no one gon'na catch me
cause I love to be free
So better watch out for my precious self, beginning now
Don't have a forwarding address for my fan mail
Tip toeing through the treacherous smiles
and the aspects of myself that do not serve me
I have dropped them off
at the station
of the cross
Thank you God for carrying me
and my little Louis purse
I am not all of my aspects
As I told you

Virginia doesn't live here any more.
and neither does the wolf.

Thank You

Thank you
for
slipping your hand
where dreams are born.

Femme Fierce: Flashes of Courage

Hey San Francisco

The bosphorous
glistened
against the evening sky
a deeper blue reflecting
the light of your eyes

Serenaded by half tone
seductive sorcery play
You spoke politics and social graces
I was far away
in a midnight oasis
we sailed the Tigres
ascendant pleasure undressing my soul slowly
small kisses lightly upon my nape
with each note another veil fell
conversations faded
crowd dispelled

Artichokes infused with fragrant oils
nibbled and licked the oil from tender leaves
like your limbs
I aspire to wrap around my tongue

We dance the dance
of the exotic
bare bellies beckon the sirens
roses fragrant wafts and weakens my defense
hand dipped chocolates melt in my mouth
like me in yours
perhaps someday
essence of bergamot
night jasmine upon you
the sweet libation
of lusty new love

Istanbul will forever have your name

emblazoned upon it
Kismet in a keepsake box
There are so few perfect moments
when love is new and your gaze squeaky clean

The soft persistence of you

Brunch

Sweet rolls freshly baking
fresh brewed coffee
love we're making
over my head
on my knees
pure confection, pass them please
And just between sips
press my lips
against your tongue
and make a wish
caramel strewn
across the sheets,
our delightful morning feast.

Coffee, crosswords, hot cakes too,
sizzling warm inside of you
am I
and you
in me
it seems
too
yummy
Yes, let's lick it clean
and help myself
to seconds
with haste
there is so much more of you to taste.

House Party at the Lake

Not sure what to wear
for dinner with my friends
Just can't resist those celebrations
kind regards and salutations
fervent glances, motions made
toward a secret hide away
far from the crowd of well worn wishers
up the stairs for stolen kisses
this old bed creeks and misses.
How many lovers has it supported
as we quite riotously contorted?

Someone's coming!
SSH!
There is some rumbling up the stairs
no one shall see
the chandelier shaking,
they'll never hear the noise we're making.

A thunderous clap and it's not storming,
the door gave way and we went rolling
on the floor and banged our heads.
Laughed till we cried
our faces red.
Smoothed my skirt
and straightened his shirt,
with presents in hand
we rejoined
the guests.
Back down the stairs
with sheepish grins
they're all played out
and we're all in.

Possess Me Not

Possess me not
Enter me often
Leave soft prints on my heart
Sear my flesh
with your tongue
and ice cream afterwards
Rock me to the blessed sleep of my ancestors
in your abundant embrace

Soar with me
in revery
through centuries of eternal lovemaking
and protect my soft curves
from the brutality of daily rituals

I beseech you
to bear down and watch
my breath
as you have your way with my innocent intentions...

Paths and epiphanies
unintrusive interpretations
leave room for you to
glissade across my lifetime
just this once
Palms touching palms
reveal your naked self to me
I shall not chuckle

In your soul I seek
a brief respit
but have no need
to occupy you

Serial Monogamy

Your eyes, pristine pools
cerilean blue skies
lapis lakes

Dolphins flirt for their own amusement
We watch
lost in them
I'd become
if it were not for your
serial love patterns
Evolve
Revolve
Resolve
Dissolve
Uninvolve

Is it a reflection of your intention
or has the rythm created a calypso collision?

Intrepid at your indications
Auditioning for a minor role in your passion play
I always play the lead you see
Usually the tragic heroine now
disclaims the debutante
falling in love with the prince rather than
the substantial seasoned sage acrobat
whose death defying stunts

go largly unnoticed...

It is your turn to choose the wine

I am addicted to the journey
of youthful glances

Broken Promises

i morn
the last scent of you
dripping from these sheets
lingering still
clinging cold and damp
like the day
its chilly in here
bleach will make them ready
for the new boy

Femme Fierce: Flashes of Courage

There Will Be No Prisoners

This uncontrollable urge
to rip the last ounce of flesh from you,
chewing it up and spitting it out
does not offend me
I am a carnivore, after all

There will be no prisoners in this turf war
only the dead
and MIA
Preferring you dead,
my anger is consumed by this passion play

Extinguish this flame by suffocating me
burn me in effigy, saint or slut, chanteuse or siren
There will be no song
covering my pain with a camoflage suit
canteen in hand and mine fields ahead

I deplore your despicable, duplicitous nature
for your sting there is no antidote
except for the kiss of the spider woman

Bubbling Up
Confessions of a Champagne Girl

I will be
eternally grateful
bubbling up
is
all we know

Champagne
a sensuous anesthesia
imperial blue
frothy white reflections
it's ether is our air

Celebrates
our rights of passage
into a certain sort of exquisite vassalage
bedazzled and beatific
appointed
to the secret and sanctimonious garden
with no desire
to move beyond
the high walls
of the beautiful life

it is the only life we know

I am grateful for
The flutes that encourage my dance
Even just for me they played and poured
And in solitude
we make sense of it all
somehow
we know
our legacy
must remain within

our gates
so sensitive to the harsh sounds
of platitude

Ode to Nike and Venus

This ode is dedicated to the iconic statues of the
Goddesses Nike of Samothrace
and Venus de Milo on display at The Louvre in Paris

Worshipped for millenniums
admirers
drawn by your imperfection and missing parts

taking comfort
and control of the features they don't see
sort of a dark macabre fantasy

this adoration of half a woman

Your
marble
visages
the perfect metaphor
for the lives we have been allowed to lead

Perfect in our lessening
Adored in our incompleteness
Worshipped in our brokenness
Feared in our beauty
Made famous after being fractured
Lithe and limbless
Decorated and decapitated
Glorified
once rendered useless
except on a pedastal
of some station or other

Fair warning given to all women who step into the fullness
of their
loving

I can imagine you both
complete and courageous
Gorgeous beyond the half witted oglers
Constant throughout time
Wise beyond the wrappings of your modesty
Strong beneath the layers of your gentility
Emancipated by understanding
Oozing from your pores
exudes the essence of your earthly tenure

Nike how you
attend to your dear sister Venus
with wings
Angels
adorned you
and a halo
of kisses
and breathlessness
enraptured by your elegant nature
And Ms. de Milo
your keen vision sears through the eons of time
guiding fair Nike to the phoenix nest
your selfless support of each halves does render you
whole

In your effigy
I see your genius
and the call to order for the coming of age of all women
We are more than our W2's
and sad soliloquys paying homage to our lacks, violations
and fears

They may have immortalized your restraint
I see your bravery

The Interview

Married?
Yes, twice

Divorced?
Yes, twice

Dating?
For decades

Children?
Yes, 3...2 living

Single Mother?
Yes, aren't we all

Grandchildren?
Yes, she is my muse or maybe I am hers

Abused?
Yes

Verbally?
Mentally?
Physically?
All of the above

Cheated on?
Yes

Lied to?
Yes

Left?
Yes

Younger men?
(:

Older men?
):

Married Men?
of course

Raped?
Yes, a grey area

Abortion?
Yes

Serial Monogamists?
Yes

Friends with benefits?
Aren't they all?

Bad Boys?
My PhD

Projects?
My other specialty

Prospects?
So many compromises, so little time

Professionals?
Yes

Alcoholics?
Yes

Narcissists?
Like a moth to the flame

Druggies?
It must have been a generational thing

Men of the Cloth?
Most of them wore clothes

Shall we pause now?
Yes

Can you do better?
Yes

Ah, but I can do younger.

I see, well then, by all means, be my guest

La Danseuse
1976

Pink Slippers upon a blue mile
danced with their satin strength
and lovely laces
made my heart's song
a sweet sin

My frolicking ceased for a while
and my slippers turned stone
soft and impressionable
my bare feet touched the earth
my hands set out to describe lesser images

And now my ballet has begun anew
a divine Swan Lake
I will offer to you my soul
with each exacting effort
and every subdued sigh

This time my pirouette will not
suffer uncertain slows
it will revolve flawlessly and forever
or
until the pink air perfects the blue dust
and the whole reflects the hollow

If God Wore A Tu Tu

If
God
wore a tutu
it
would be pink

Dearest Children

I am grateful for so many things
so many marvelous moments of God's grace and
goodness in this life
never more thankful
for the present of you both in my world

Gentle children
warriors of wisdom
kind caring souls
knowers of truth
soldiers of righteousness
patriots of freedoms
caretakers of the mute
helpless
creatures

Children of mine
sucked at my breast
the sheer wonder of you
amazes me

As you round the bend
toward adulthood
I am in awe
of your
discrete knowledge
and inner beauty

Proud of your discernment
God given and fleshed out
sweeps me away

Don't ever lose yourself
accept to the Spirit
save for the epiphanies
that call you to duty each day

As I grow tired
take care of the other children
in this weary world
no matter how many years they wear
we all need care

With all the strength of my heart
and the courage of my convictions

Through the enormous failings of my character
I love you perfectly

Little Boy Blue

Earth and sand
carefully collected
your small cup
spilling
over
running
helter skelter
so eager
to show me your wares
Now constellations
create your map
kisses flow
from your cappucino and latte love stars

I will be the Sunday call
lucky enough to be a
priviledged witness
to your taller shaven reflection

Torch
passes
illuminating
alternate actual paths to self
My only participation now
is eager audience member

Oh my dear
baby blue
boy
Wiping your yummyliscious mouth
as a napkin, my shoulder
Playing peek a boo behind my skirt
crumpled up in your palms
a life line to your sky

Allonsy, Allez
Rush toward yourself standing still prepared for the leap

Hold your hand a bit higher please
I
want
to see you
rise

Gina

Intuitive
feeler of all moments
Your laughter
fairies
dancing
Your grace
angelic elegance
Your heart
Jesus' embrace to all who are hurting
Your beauty
Eternal Light

Your profile
regal
belying the tiny years of your child eyes gazing
reserved and enigmatic
shielding you
from the assault
noxious fumes and startling revelations

Loyal without compromise
Brave in every step
Virtuous in every comment
Careful in every consideration
Fiery
Naive
Wise
Rebellious
all at the same time
mercurial
My daughter
There will never be another one like you

Take care
Be yourself
Risk it

She is counting on you
we all are
praying
for you
to accept the
challenge
Become your highest
best self
There is no other path for us

I will walk beside you
behind you
in front of you
but I cannot walk within you

My daughter
My soul's soul
My first breath
My last kiss
My hearts desire
My gift to you
is life
My promise to you
is to hold you safe
My wish for you is to find joy and peace
My prayer for you is
to discover
that you are
Love
Perfect and precious
At every glance
And to know that regardless of your path
your journey
will always lead you home.

Just One Thing Before I Go

Just one thing before I go,
I have loved you
with the kiss of the Infinite
upon your soft ticklish tummy

Swaddled you
in this crushable aging cashmere skin
and silk heart strands
of the Holy One

Quieted your wanting wails
while
whispering away the cares of this bright harsh world
with lullabies
where all my secrets I did pour in

Just one thing before I go,
I want to tell you
This love has come through me
as the joy
of eternity's fair glances
upon your smiling face
the same as it will always be

You are the angels' muse
for every mother whose child
she watches dreaming
while gazing into the stars
She wonders,
how many sleeps will I awaken from
and still see
the cherub's eyes?

Just one more thing before I go,
it was through me
that your first cry for love leapt

from my womb
echoing from the
inside out
in my pacing to calm you

And it is from me
in the humanness
of the full and passionate coupling of our hearts
will forever be entwined

Just one thing before I go,
I implore you to keep your wild heart
longing
and free
from all that might restrain your desire to live

Rise to the ebb and flow of
Heaven's breezes
Let the silvery moon
tug at your banana curled dirty blond hair

Keep looking up.

For one that would cage you
will never desire God's heart for you.

His heart for you is to only love
and live
abundantly

Your journey will be precious.
Love all that he has created for you
so that for your joy to be full

And just one more thing before I go,
I will share a simple secret with you my beloved

Tug at my sleeve forever

Pursue all of my attention,
don't you see..
you will always be
the center of my universe...

We will never be apart from each other
No matter
the vanishing of skin into the ether,
my eyes will still twinkle

Just look to the stars
effervesce like fluted champagne
the bubbles of joy
tickle your nose
and
quench your thirst
with the everlasting spirit of Divine love

I will be holding
your tiny eager fragrant powdered hand
in the palm of my grateful heart
smiling with you

For in the moment
as in all moments born in God's love... there is only joy

Listen
In the midnight sky
you will hear me laughing
until the day
our spirit will join in a single embrace
and together
we shall bubble up

About Mary

Mary Giuseffi has been a strong voice and advocate for women, children and the misunderstood, all her life. She is a Poet in motion. No matter what medium she chooses to explore…it is unmistakably art in action. She has worked within the layers of transformational space since childhood. Relationships are her life and breadth. Mary intimately understands and communicates the essence of relationships of all kinds and with all matter. Her gift is to explore the beauty, passion and nuances of our life experiences and express their emotional, spiritual, intellectual and physical facets in many modalities.

It all started with a little orange box when she was 5 years old, collecting change for UNICEF…she became intimately aware that not all children lived the love filled and sweet life of her carefree childhood. Since then she has worked with abused and abandoned children one on one, created programs and safe havens as well as raised millions of dollars for their protection and benefit. She even created an event that raised over a quarter of a million dollars for UNICEF and worked with Audrey Hepburn…her childhood mentor.

Mary has fearlessly worked on behalf of women for over 30 years. Her first book, Too Much Rain an abortion journal, bravely addressed the rights of women to own their bodies and the need for the Catholic Church to provide programming to heal aborted women. She worked with hundreds of women who had never shared their secret. She even testified on the floor of the United States Senate, as her letter was read supporting young women in crisis. Her poetry and prose exposed the deep wounds of women caught amid the Roe vs. Wade decision being a guest on 48 hrs. with Tom Brokaw, a speaker, work shop facilitator and performance artist.

While living in Chicago, Mary was trained to be a Rape Victim Advocate. She said it was the most difficult thing she had ever experienced. Being alone in a hospital room with a woman who had just been brutally raped.

Mary has worked on all sides of the camera since childhood. She was a Ford Model in New York City, a teenage opera singer and actress. Later she became the creative director for her own production company that created spectacular performance art pieces, runway fashion shows and extraordinary visceral events. She spoke nationwide on self-image, dressing for success and how to create a beautiful life. She graduated 10,000 young people from her etiquette and self-esteem programs from country club kids to juvenile delinquents, Mary shared her love and joy and powerful knowledge inspiring them to succeed in life through respect, discipline and humor.

Giuseffi received many awards through the years for her dedication and commitment to many charitable institutions in South Florida, where she resided for almost thirty years, including Woman of The Year, Volunteer of the Year, Women of Style and Substance, Outstanding Women of Broward County to name a few.

Fast-forward to today, Mary's most recent book, Straight Up With A Twist, has become an Amazon #1 Best Seller. She has enjoyed great success in the area of relationship expertise and has appeared on The Today Show with Kathie Lee and Hoda several times. She put a whimsical spin on her female empowerment platform and created a guide for self-actualization and finding love and romance by discovering your cocktail personality. Men and women have truly loved this pithy and fun read. Its empowerment message does not go unnoticed. It's honest and straightforward.

Mary also has spearheaded her own consulting firm which deals with how people "show up in the world". Her personal branding, marketing strategies, laser sharp intuition and extraordinary taste has successfully launched authors, entrepreneurs and professionals to stardom and best seller status while increasing profitability and notability in their respective fields. She is clearly a coach's coach in transformational circles.

Mary speaks and performs world wide on the subjects that are near and dear to her heart, "Our future relies upon creating an entirely new feminine paradigm for governing, based upon inclusion, cooperation and compassion. We cannot cobble together a viable vision from a tree that not longer bears fruit. We must embrace the essential nature of being female and precede fearlessly arm in arm, side-by-side, back-to-back, lifting each other up and expanding in Love."

Mary currently lives in Marina Del Rey, California and West Palm Beach, Florida. She has two grown children and a granddaughter, Arielle, her muse.